Just Handwriting
Pre-cursive Handwriting F
1st Class

educate.ie

Authors: Gráinne Keating and Sarah McCarthy
Editor: Susan McKeever
Design: Philip Ryan Graphic Design
Illustration: Peter Wilks
© 2012 Educate.ie, Castleisland, County Kerry, Ireland.
ISBN: 978-1-908507-15-0

Printed in Ireland by Walsh Colour Print, Castleisland, County Kerry. Freephone 1800 613 111.

Without limiting the rights under copyright, this book is sold subject to the condition that it shall not, by way of trade or otherwise, be lent, resold, hired out, reproduced, stored in or introduced into a retrieval system, or transmitted, in any form or by any means (electronic, mechanical, photocopying, recording or otherwise), or otherwise circulated, without the publisher's prior consent, in any form other than that in which it is published and without a similar condition being imposed on the subsequent publisher. The author and publisher have made every effort to trace all copyright holders, but if some have been inadvertently overlooked we would be happy to make the necessary arrangements at the first opportunity.

Contents

Introduction	2	Letter 'j'	23	Letters 'V, W'	44
Let's Get Ready!	3	Letter 'l'	24	Letters 'I, L'	45
Letter 'c'	4	Letter 't'	25	Revising 'V, W, I, L'	46
Letter 'o'	5	Letter 'b'	26	Letters 'H, A'	47
Letter 'a'	6	Revising 'i, j, l, t, b'	27	Letters 'T, Y'	48
Letter 'd'	7	Letter 'p'	28	Revising 'H, A, T, Y'	49
Letter 'g'	8	Letter 'k'	29	Letters 'K, X'	50
Letter 'q'	9	Revising 'p, k'	30	Letters 'F, E'	51
Revising 'c, o, a, d, g, q'	10	Letter 'f'	31	Revising 'K, X, F, E'	52
Letter 'u'	11	Letter 'v'	32	Letters 'N, M'	53
Letter 'y'	12	Letter 'w'	33	Letters 'U, J'	54
Revising 'u, y'	13	Letter 'x'	34	Revising 'N, M, U, J'	55
Letter 'h'	14	Letter 'z'	35	Letters 'D, P'	56
Letter 'r'	15	Revising 'f, v, w, x, z'	36	Letters 'B, R'	57
Letter 'n'	16	Practice	37	Revising 'D, P, B, R'	58
Letter 'm'	17	Congratulations!	38	Practice	59
Revising 'h, r, n, m'	18	Let's Move!	39	Practice	60
Letter 's'	19	Letters 'C, O'	40	Practice	61–62
Letter 'e'	20	Letters Q, G'	41	Mirror Drawing	63
Revising 's, e'	21	Letters 'S, Z'	42	Handwriting Certificate	64
Letter 'i'	22	Revising 'C, O, G, Q, S, Z'	43		

Introduction

The **Just Handwriting** series consists of:
Just Handwriting: Early Years (3-4 years)
Just Handwriting: Early Years (4-5 years)
Just Handwriting Script: Junior Infants to Second Class. (Includes a practice copy for each class.)
Just Handwriting Cursive: Junior Infants to Sixth Class. (Includes a practice copy for each class from Junior Infants to Second Class.)

The aim of the programme is to enable children to write fluently, comfortably, quickly and legibly. Handwriting is a form of communication and one on which we are often judged.

Remember the Four Ps: Preparation, Pencil Grip, Posture, Practice.

Preparation (Junior Infants to Second Class): The simple, fun 'Let's Get Ready!' exercises help to relax the child mentally and physically and enable them to focus on the planned activity. Encourage the child to draw or trace the 'Giant Sunglasses' before every writing activity. In time, it will become part of their work routine.

Pencil Grip: The correct pencil grip will lead to quick, fluent writing.

Posture: Good posture helps the writing stamina of the child.

Practice: The formation of each letter is clearly illustrated so the child will have a reference that shows him or her how to form each letter, especially if more than one stroke is involved. Handwriting is an essential skill that needs to be taught and fluency only comes with plenty of practice. Practice, practice, practice makes perfect and enables the child to become a confident writer.

Assessment

There is a self-assessment option at the bottom of each page. The child ticks the face that they feel applies to their completion of the page.

Individual Books (Pre-cursive to Cursive Version)

Junior Infants Book: This book focuses on the correct formation of all lowercase letters. The letters are pre-cursive (with 'tails'). This level also includes a practice copy; this focuses on the formation of lowercase letters, and can be used at the teacher's discretion.

Senior Infants and First Class Books: These books focus on the correct formation of all uppercase letters as well as further practice in lowercase. Both books include a practice copy, focusing on capital letters, that can be used at the teacher's discretion.

Second Class Book: In the Second Class book the width of the lines changes from 6mm to 5mm from Page 39 onwards in preparation for third class. All writing exercises are meaningful e.g. recipes, quiz-style questions and answers and interesting facts. (Includes a practice copy.)

Third to Sixth Class (Cursive Writing)

Third Class Book: This is the stage where children are introduced to cursive looped writing. They will discover that many of the lowercase letters are unchanged from those that have been taught already. Most of the remaining letters involve loops. Later in the year the capital letters are introduced.

Fourth Class Book: Now the children begin to write using a pen. An inexpensive cartridge pen with a fine-pointed nib or a fine-pointed fibre pen (not felt) is recommended. Under no circumstances should a biro or a ballpoint pen be used. In fact these types of pens should not be used for writing in any primary school class.

The Fifth Class Book: Lower and uppercase letters are repeated from Pages 3 to 11 to revise, reinforce and provide practice of correct letter formation. The most important writing rules are repeated throughout the book. Pupils should use the same pen suggested in the Fourth Class book. The contents of this book vary from facts, stories and poetry to dictionary exercises and legends.

The Sixth Class Book: Lower and uppercase letters from Pages 3 to 8 provide revision of letter formation. Once again the writing rules are repeated throughout the book. The first half of the book has blue and red lines; the second half of the book has double blue lines for 12 pages and 'copy' lines for the last 12 pages. Pupils are recommended to use the same type of pen as they used in Fourth and Fifth Class. There is a variety of material in this book – factual pieces, legends, riddles, stories and tongue twisters.

Let's Get Ready!

Wake Up!
1. Gently 'wash your face' using your fingers.
2. Tap gently around your eyes.
3. Tug at the top of your ears. Tug at the middle of your ears. Tug at your earlobes.
4. Massage your jaw. Get rid of those yawns.
5. Take a deep breath and lift your shoulders to your ears. Breathe out and drop your shoulders.

Pencil Grip

Don't squeeze me! Hold me!
Put your pencil down on the desk. The point of your pencil should be facing your tummy. Bring down your writing hand. Use your thumb and forefinger to pick up your pencil. Push the pencil back into the 'valley' of your hand.

Checklist
This panel appears throughout the book to remind children to: **1.** Wake up!, **2.** Check their posture (chair in, feet down, back straight, don't frown) and **3.** Check their pencil grip.

Wake up!	Posture	Pencil grip

Giant Sunglasses
1. Trace over the 'sunglasses' with your finger.
2. Trace over the 'sunglasses' with your pencil.

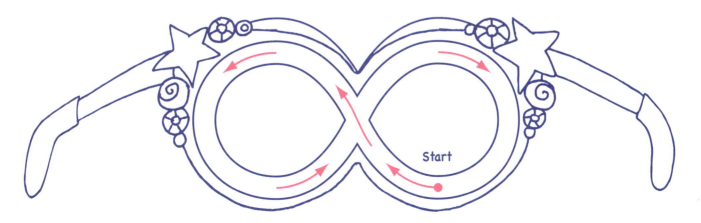

o

Chair in,
Feet down,
Back straight,
Don't frown.

Tues o o o o o o o o o

Wed

on off one oh odd
of out ox old okay
once o'clock or our

a

a a a a a a a a

a
a
a
a
a

able ace act add

age aim air all and

ant any are arm art

d

**Chair in,
Feet down,
Back straight,
Don't frown.**

d d d d d d d d d

d

d

d

d

d

do dog dad did

dig door down

draw doll dolphin

q

q never walks alone: qu

Chair in,
Feet down,
Back straight,
Don't frown.

q q q q q q q q

quad   quake   queen

quest   question   quiet

quick   quill   quilt

REVISE

coadgq

coadgq coadgq

cat   coal   act   dad

go   queen   clap

off   add   doll   good

10

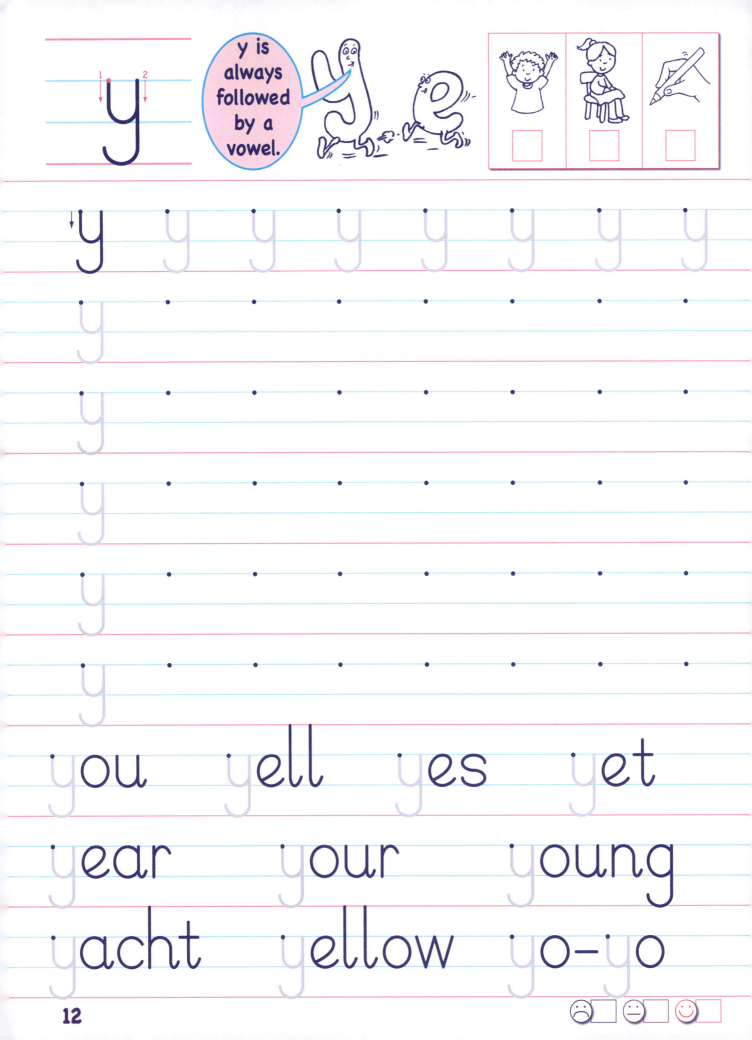

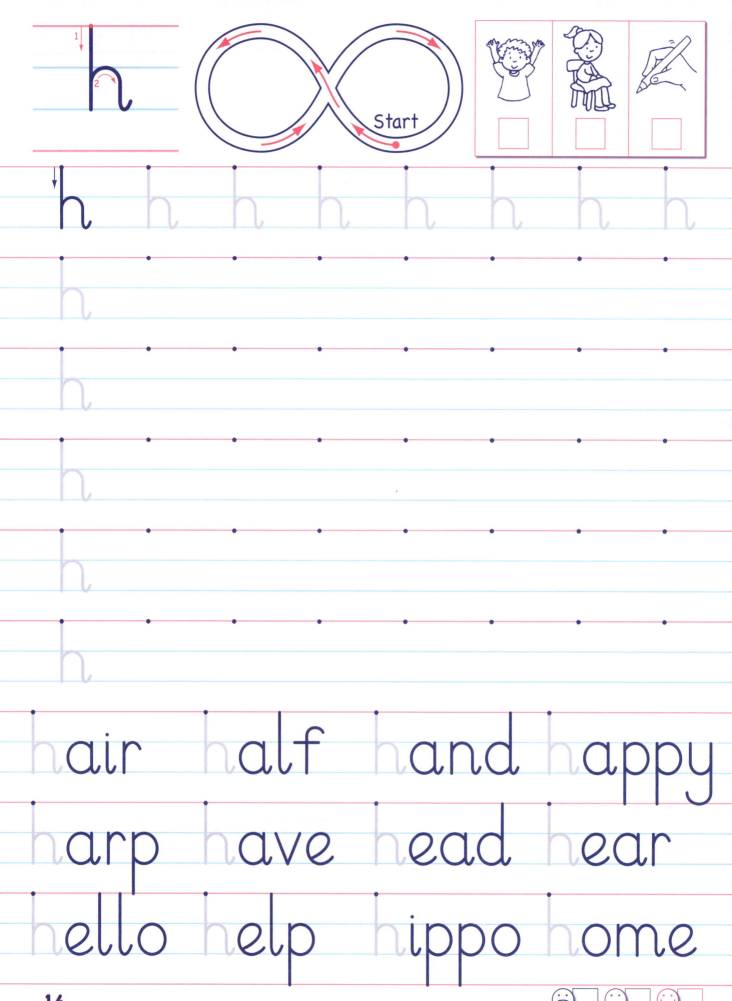

m

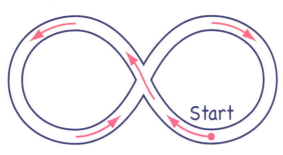

**Chair in,
Feet down,
Back straight,
Don't frown.**

m m m m m m m m m

m

m

m

m

m

made magic main make

map mark mask march

match milk mind moon

REVISE

h r n m

hug　rain　number

mum　heart　rabbit

nail　mummy　ham

18

s

Chair in,
Feet down,
Back straight,
Don't frown.

s

sack safe sail sand
school second see-saw
slide slither snake

e

e e e e e e e e e

e

e

e

e

e

ear   egg   eye   ewe
eight eighteen eighty
eve   extra   email

s e

Chair in,
Feet down,
Back straight,
Don't frown.

s e s e s e s e

seven   seventeen

seventy   seventy-seven

sell   sew   send   seed

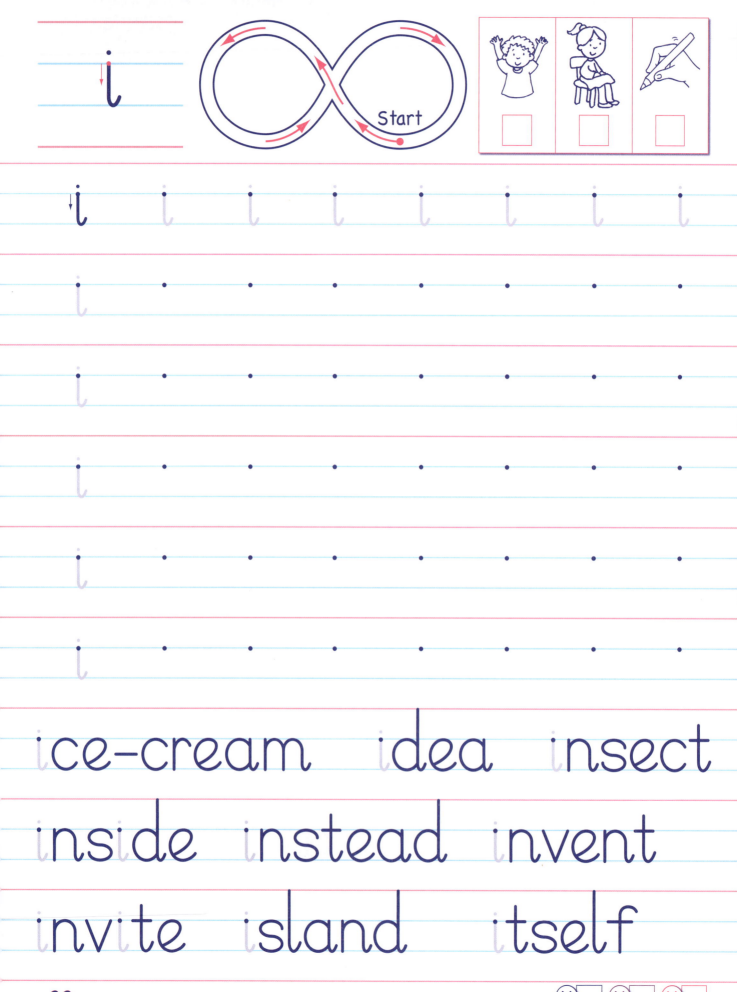

ice-cream idea insect

inside instead invent

invite island itself

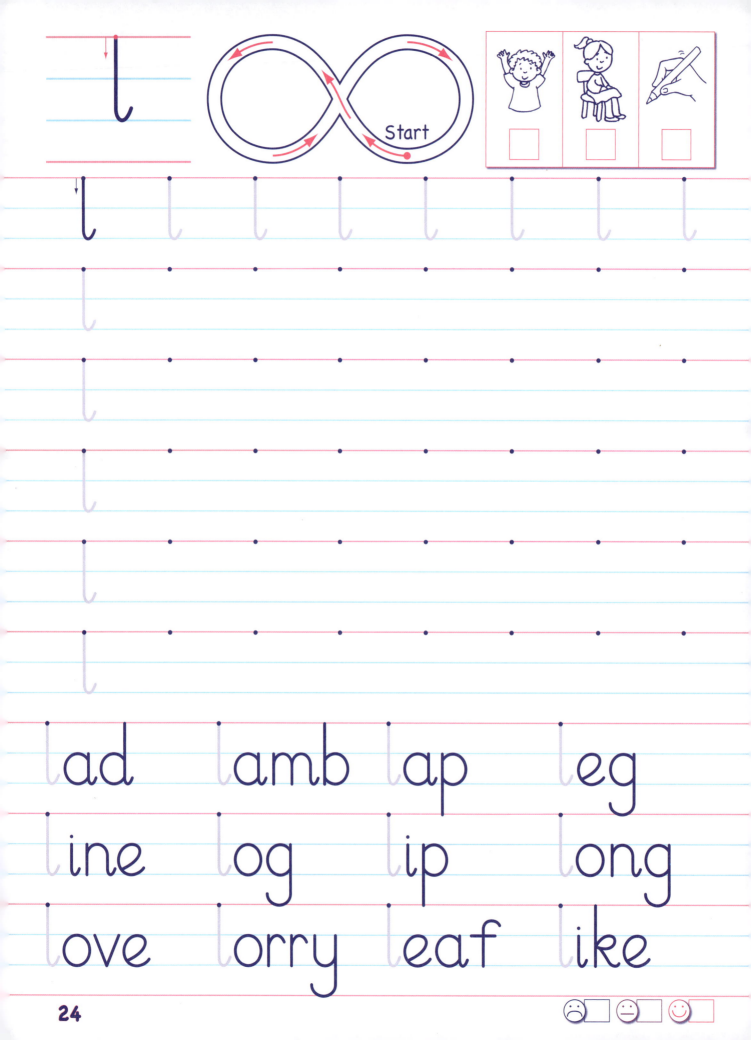

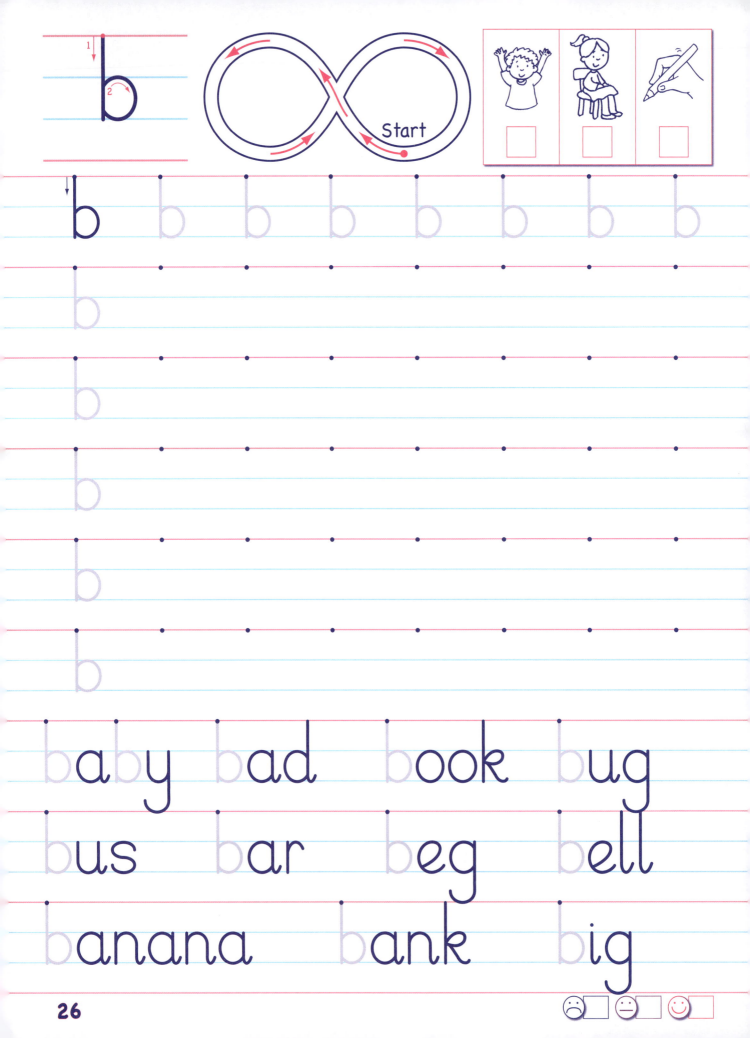

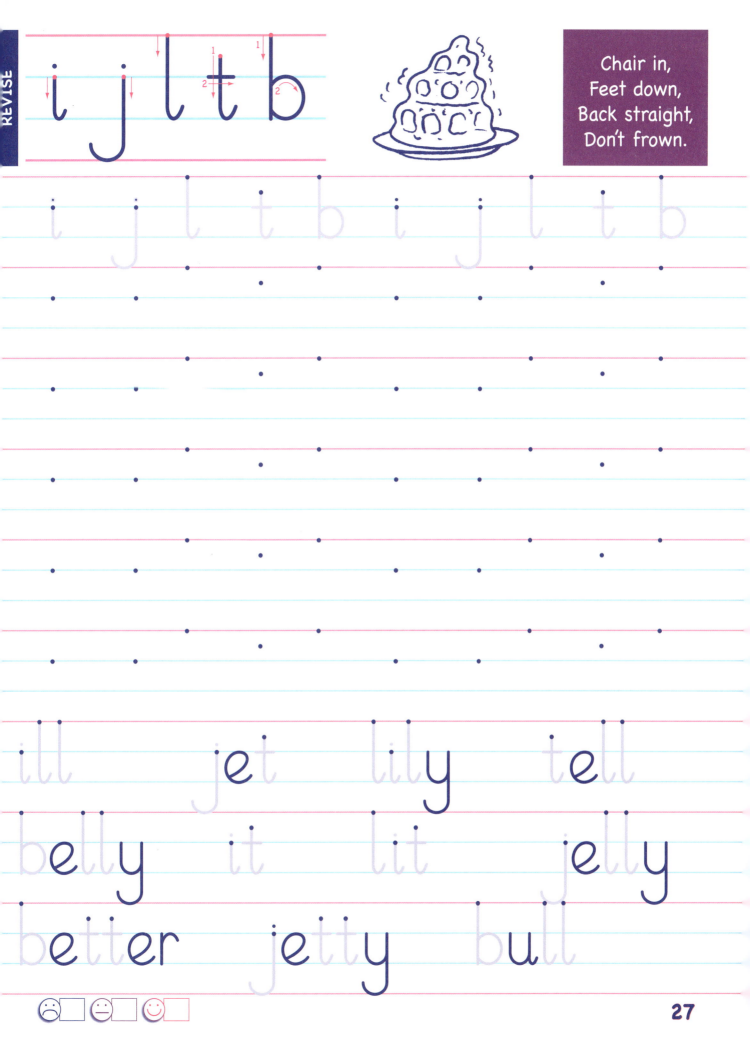

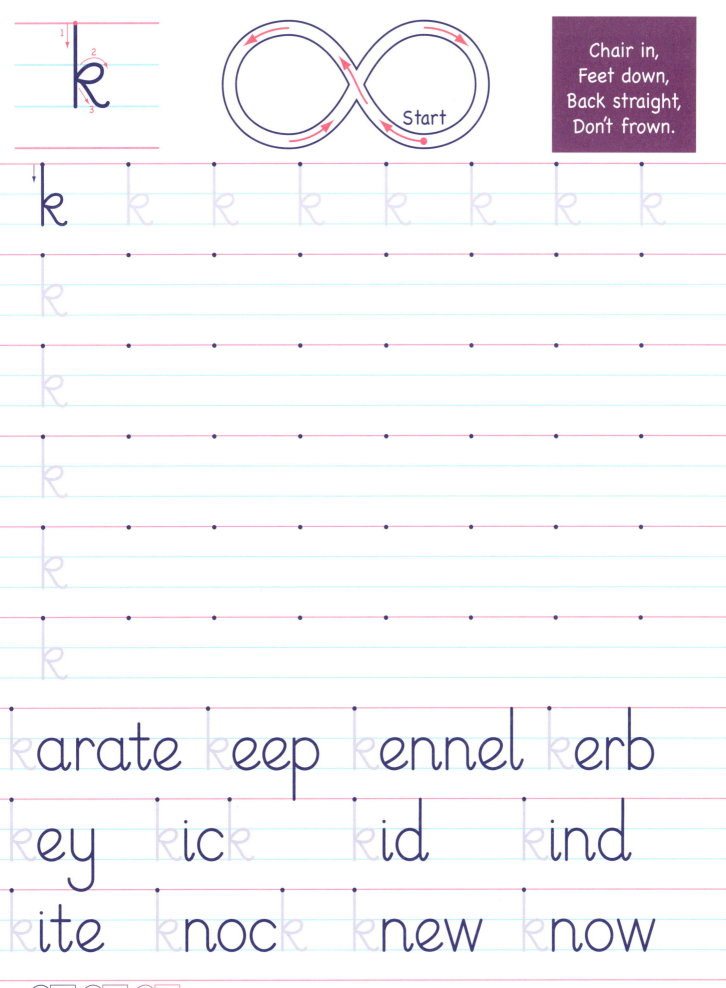

Chair in,
Feet down,
Back straight,
Don't frown.

karate keep kennel kerb
key kick kid kind
kite knock knew know

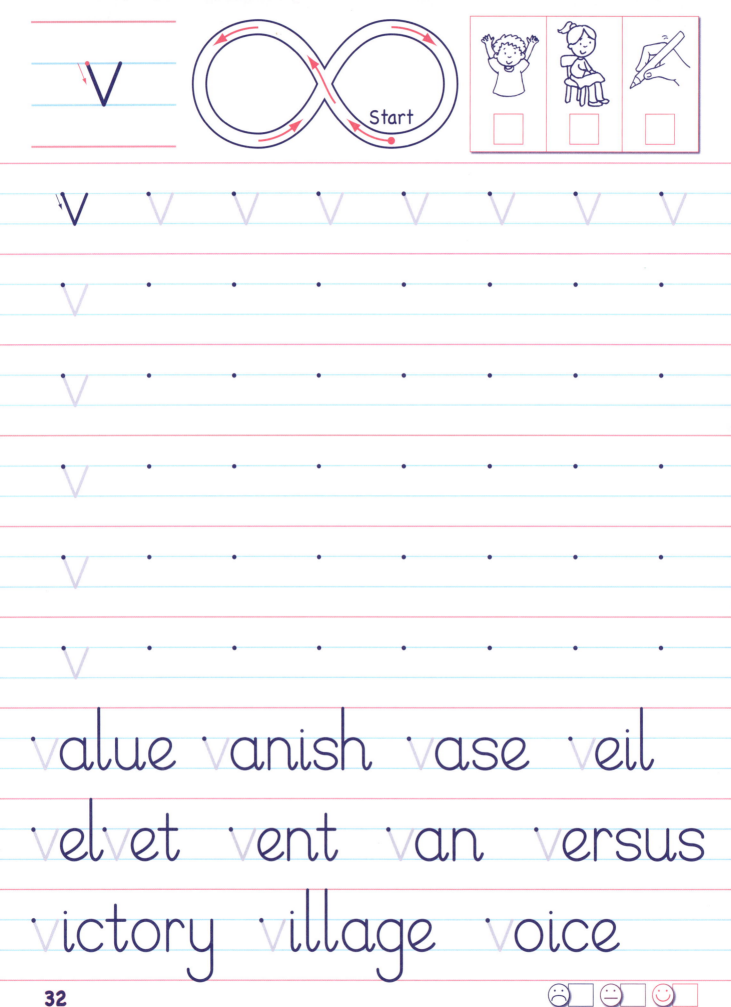

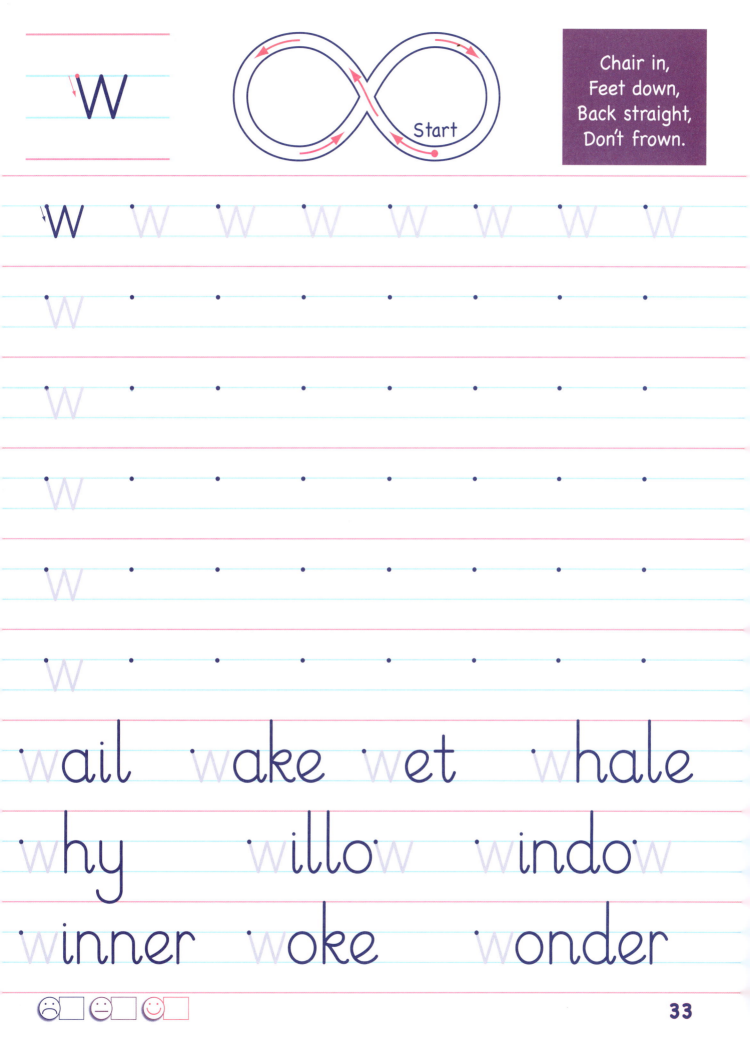

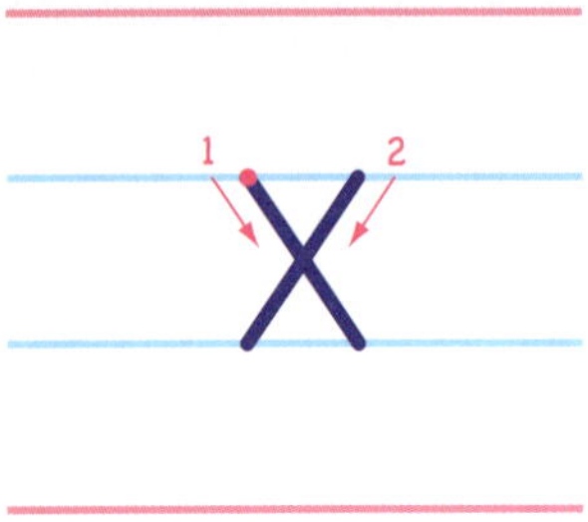

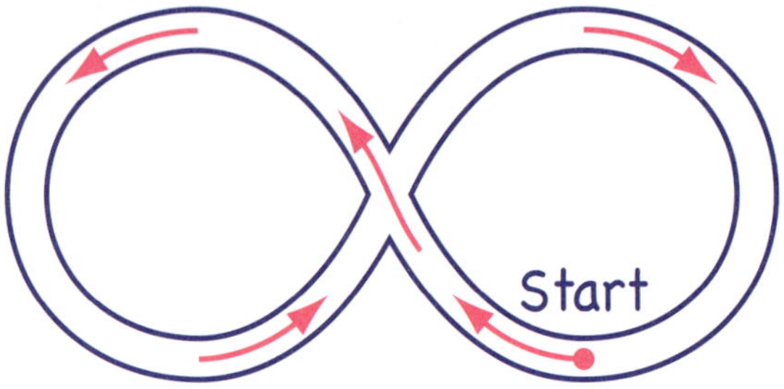

x-ray   extra   Max
Maxine   excite   exit
exercise   exam   explain

z

Chair in,
Feet down,
Back straight,
Don't frown.

z z z z z z z z z

z
z
z
z
z

zap zebra zero zest
zig zag zinc zip
zombie zone zoo zoom

35

REVISE

f v w x z f v w x z

few flex wax vixen

fax fox fix fuzz

wolf wonderful wave

36

Practice

Chair in,
Feet down,
Back straight,
Don't frown.

c o a d g q h n m

c · · · · · · · ·

i j l t b u y s e p k

i · · · · · · · · · ·

· r v w x z r v w x z r v w x z

a b c d e f g h i j k l m

a · · · · · · · · · · · ·

n o p q r s t u v w x y z

n · · · · · · · · · · · ·

37

Congratulations!

You have finished the lowercase alphabet. Well done!

I am good at writing.

I

I like to write stories.

I

Sky Writing
Draw a letter in the air. Ask others to guess the letter. Now trace a letter/word on your friend's back/palm/back of hand.

Word Pictures
Write a word and add features.

Let's Move! Activities you can do at your desk.

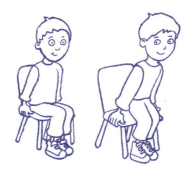

Armchair Lifts
Push your body up from your seat.

Opposites
Place your right index finger on the right side of your nose.
Place your left index finger on the left side of your nose.
Cross your right finger on your left ear.
Cross your left finger on your right ear.
Continue down the body.

Do and Say!
Nose, cross
Ears, cross
Shoulders, cross
Hips, cross
Knees, cross
Ankles, cross
Work your way
back up the body
to your nose.
Well done!

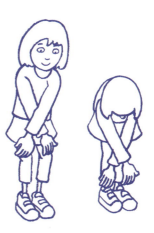

Let's Play
Work in a group or in pairs. Give the instruction.
Return to the starting position each time.
Right hand, left ear
Left hand, right elbow. Continue.
Stand opposite your partner and mirror the action.
No talking – just LOOK and MIRROR or copy.
Concentrate – relax, breathe and have fun!

COQGSZ

> Chair in,
> Feet down,
> Back straight,
> Don't frown.

C O Q C O Q C O Q

G S Z G S Z G S Z

Conor   Clive   Quentin

Grainne   Sarah   Zoe

Cathal   Orla   Sue   Zach

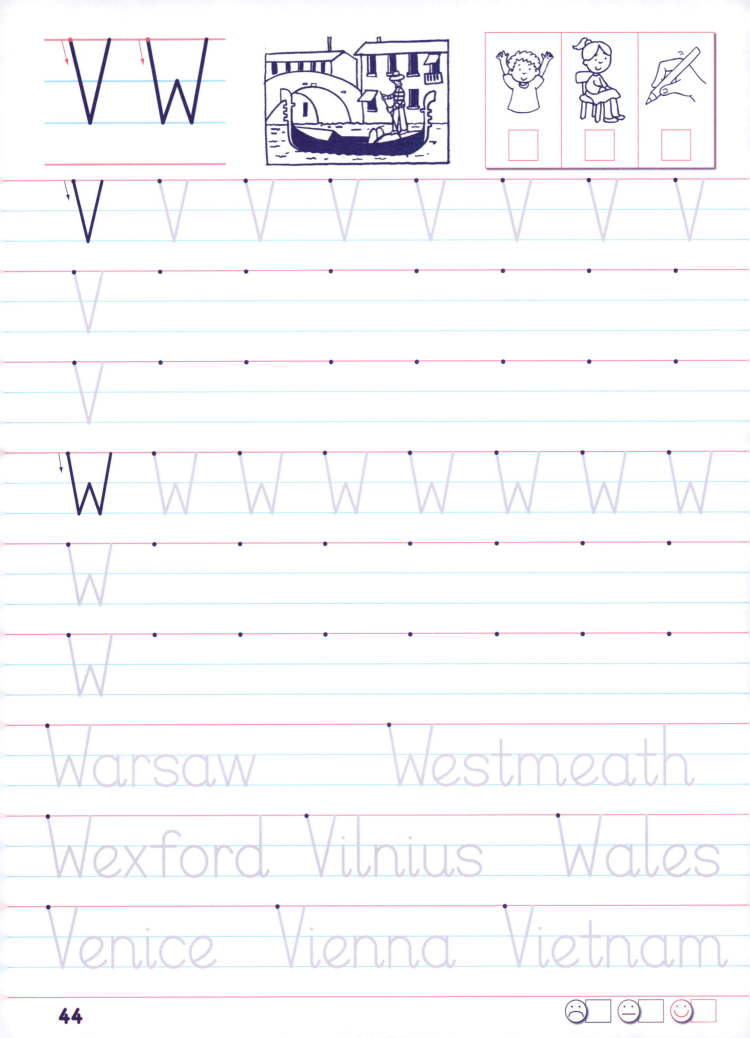

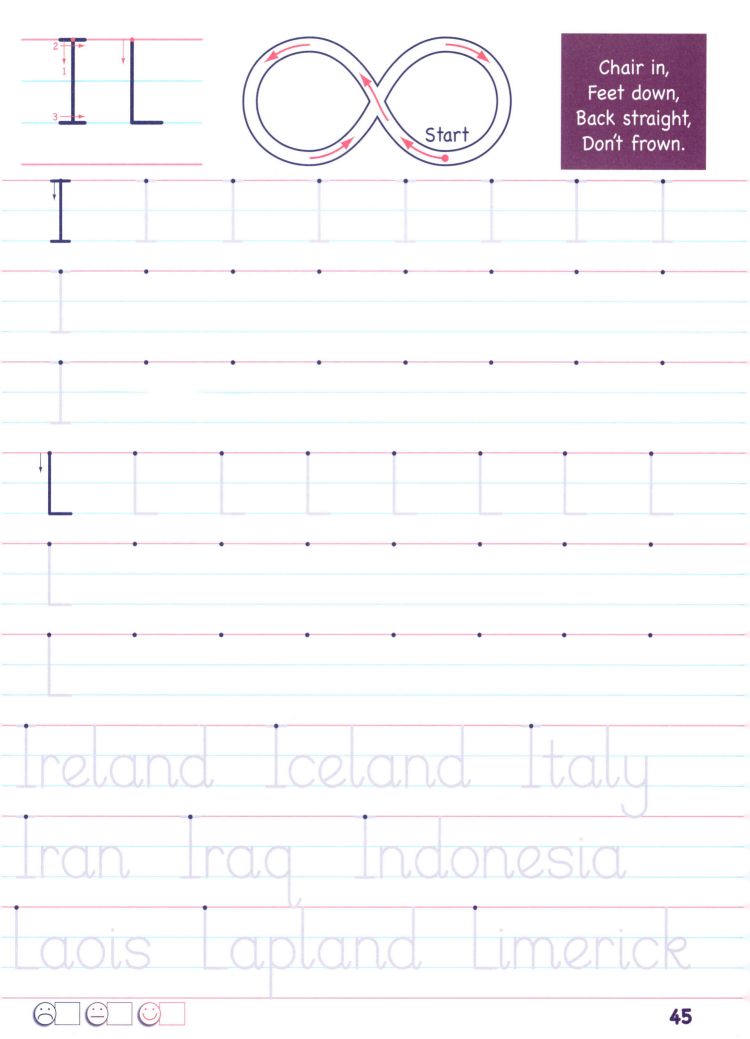

Chair in,
Feet down,
Back straight,
Don't frown.

Ireland Iceland Italy
Iran Iraq Indonesia
Laois Lapland Limerick

REVISE

VWIL

VWIL VWIL VWIL

V
V
V
V
V

Liam Ian Wendy Violet
Lucy William Victor
Imelda Laura Veronica

46

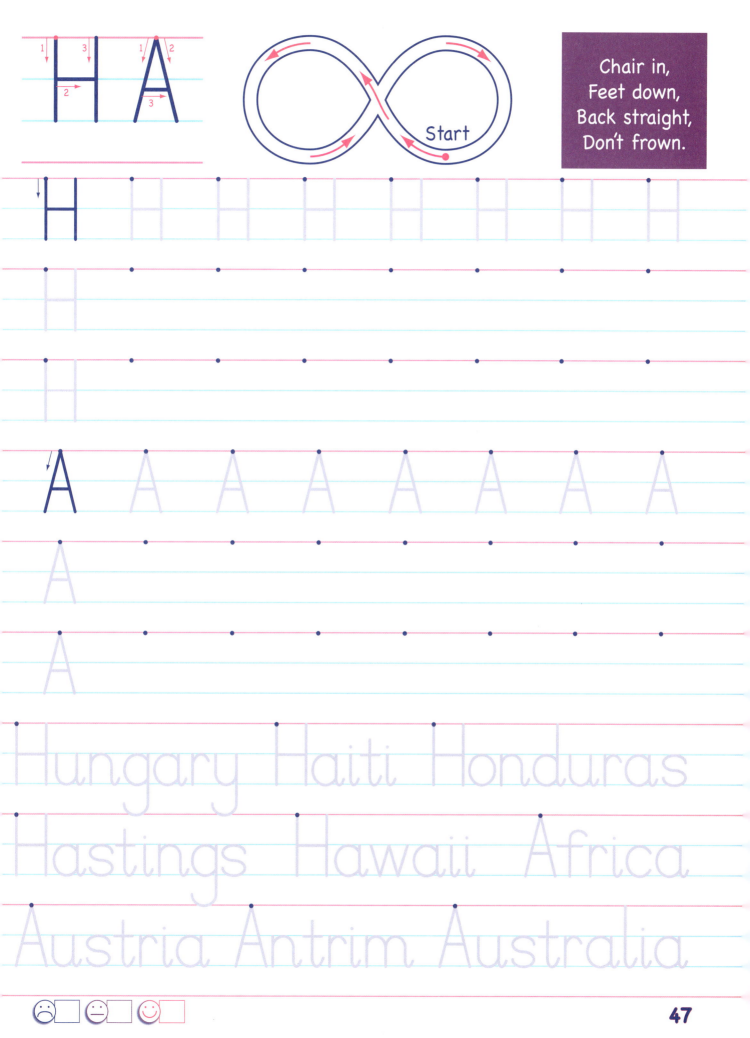

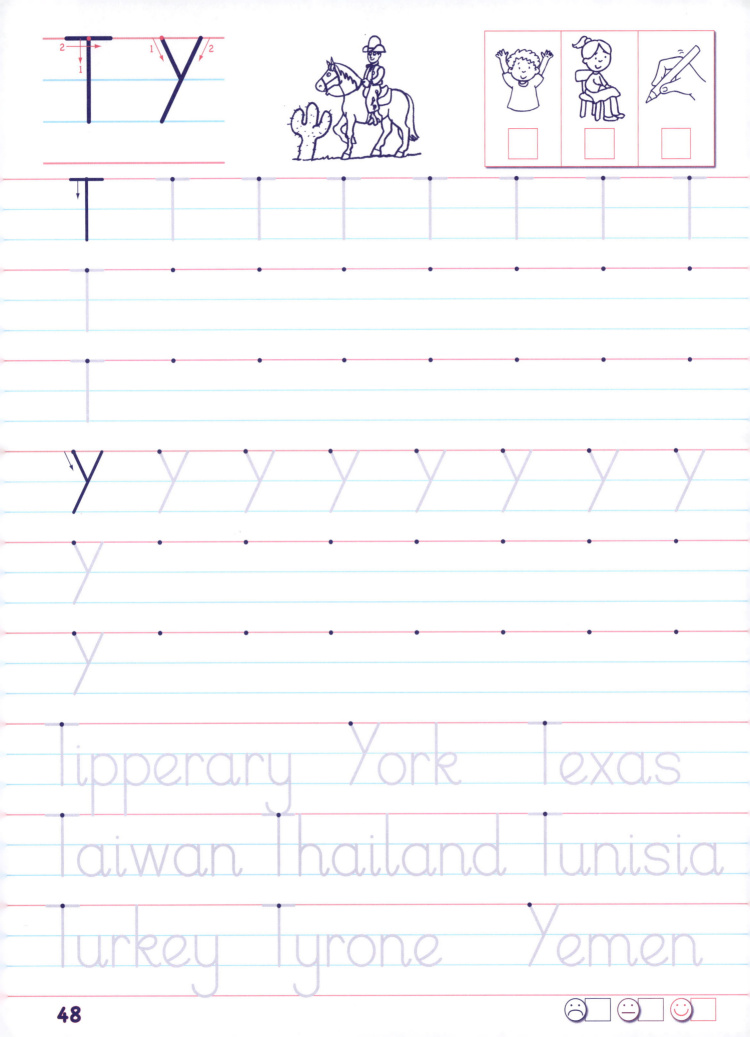

Tipperary York Texas
Taiwan Thailand Tunisia
Turkey Tyrone Yemen

HATY

Chair in,
Feet down,
Back straight,
Don't frown.

HATY HATY HATY

H
H
H
H
H
H

Harry Andrea Thomas
Yvonne Aoife Timothy
Hannah Alan Tara Helen

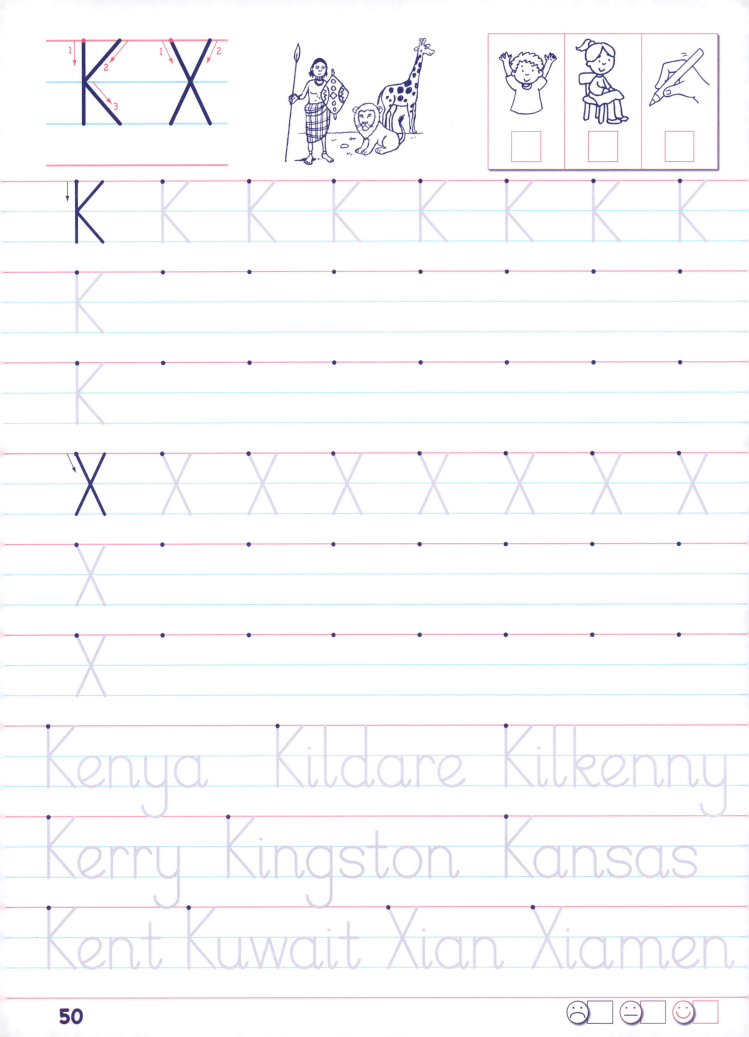

Chair in,
Feet down,
Back straight,
Don't frown.

Fermanagh Fiji Finland
France Ecuador Egypt
Eritrea Estonia Ethiopia

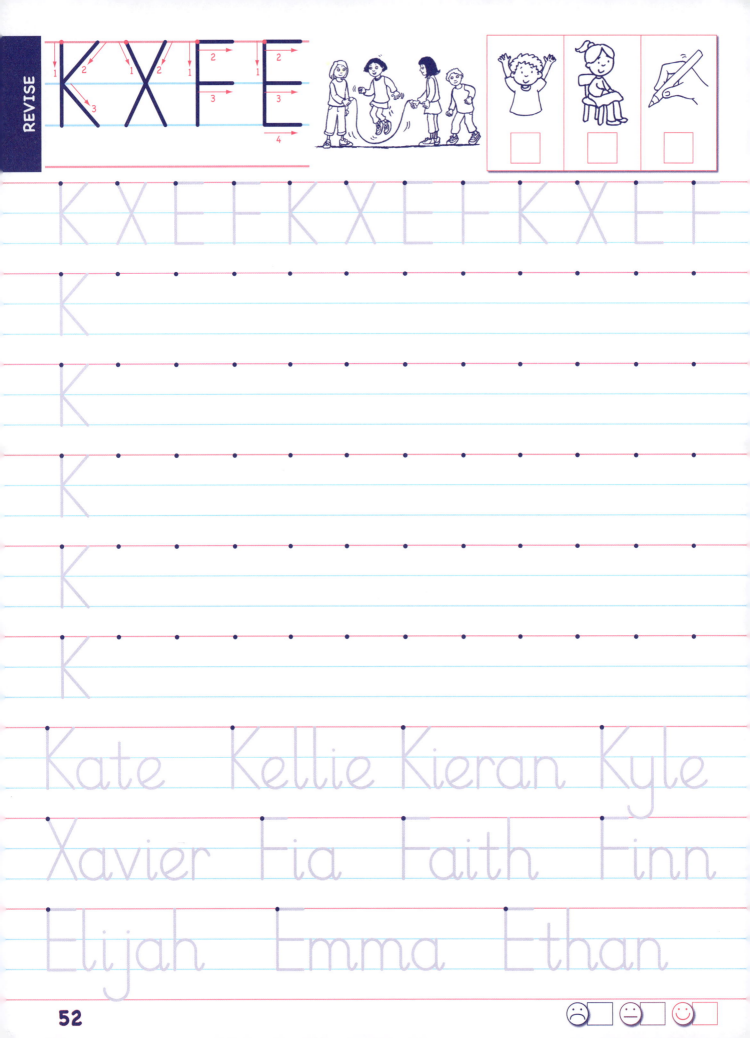

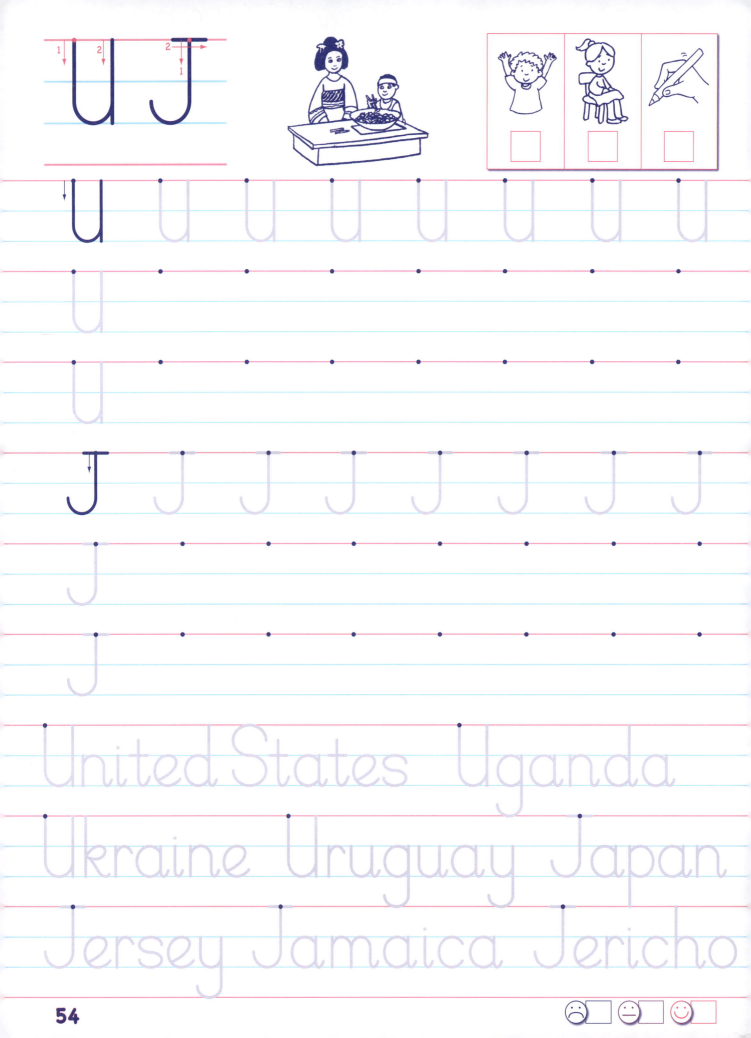

United States Uganda
Ukraine Uruguay Japan
Jersey Jamaica Jericho

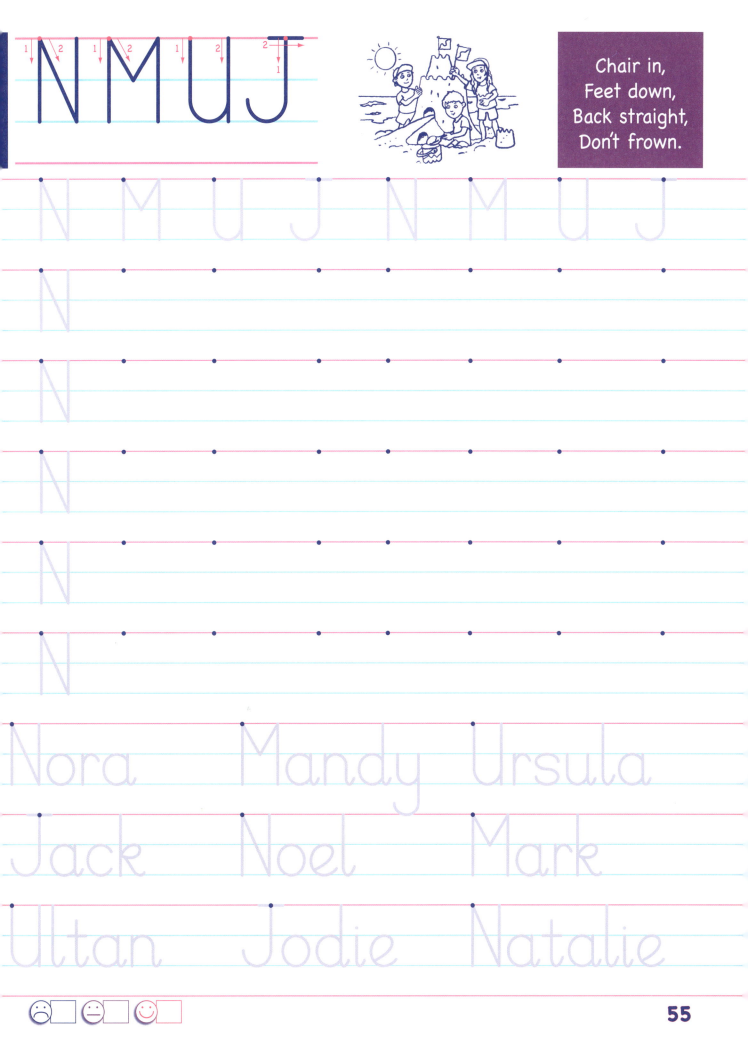

REVISE

D P B R

Dan   Patrick   Billy

Rachel   Daisy   Ruby

Rory   Duncan   Pam

Practice

Chair in,
Feet down,
Back straight,
Don't frown.

C O Q G S Z V W I L

C

H A I Y K X F E N M U J

H

D P B R D P B R D P B R

A B C D E F G H I J K L M

A

N O P Q R S T U V W X Y Z

N

Practice

Looking back at all letters.

a A b B c C d D e E f F g G

a G

h H i I j J k K l L m M n N

h N

o O p P q Q r R s S t T

o T

u U v V w W x X y Y z Z

u Z

Practice

**Chair in,
Feet down,
Back straight,
Don't frown.**

All About Me

My name is:

M   .

I am   years old.

I   .

I live in   .

I   .

I am in   class.

I

Practice

I have _____ hair.

I

I have _____ eyes.

I

My hobby is _____.

M

I love

I

I am great at handwriting

Mirror Drawing

1. A vertical line is drawn for you in the centre of the page.
2. Place a pencil in each hand and let your imagination lead you.
3. Be creative!
4. Move both hands at the same time but in opposite directions.
5. RELAX, breathe and enjoy!
6. Hint: if the page is moving, tape it to the desk.
7. Try to mirror draw with your eyes closed!

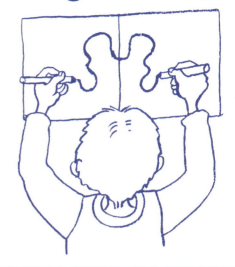

Have a go!

I am very good at writing upper and lowercase letters.

Signed:

Pupil: _____

Teacher: _____

Date: _____

CABRAMATTA / CUDMIRRAH

Jennifer Harrison

Black Pepper

© Jennifer Harrison 1996

First published by *Black Pepper*
403 St Georges Road, North Fitzroy, Victoria 3068

All rights reserved

National Library of Australia
Catalogue - in - Publication data:

Harrison, Jennifer, 1955 - .
    Cabramatta / Cudmirrah

    ISBN 1 876 044 11 X.

    I. Title.

A823.3

Cover design: Gail Hannah

 This project has been assisted by the Commonwealth Government through the Australia Council, its art funding and advisory body.

Printed and bound by Currency Productions
79 Leveson Street, North Melbourne, Victoria 3051

Jennifer Harrison was born in Liverpool, Sydney in 1955. Her previous publications include *Mosaics & Mirrors: Composite Poems* (with Graham Henderson and KF Pearson, Black Pepper, 1995) and *michelangelo's prisoners* (Black Pepper, 1995); *michelangelo's prisoners* won the 1995 Anne Elder Award and was commended in the National Book Council's Banjo Awards in the same year. She lives with her family in Melbourne where she practises as a psychiatrist.

Acknowledgments

Acknowledgement is made to the *Cafe Review*, USA, for publishing earlier versions of the poems "Headland", "Stingray" and "Thermocline".

Nine of the Cudmirrah poems were collectively commended in the 1994 Premier's Poetry Award (Warana Writers' Week, Queensland).

The following texts are acknowledged for their usefulness in researching the Cudmirrah poems: *Oceanography,* Third Edition by M. Grant Gross; *Life and Death in the Coral Sea* by Jacques-Yves Cousteau; *History of Shoalhaven* by William Bayley; *Aboriginal Words and Place Names* by A. W. Reed; *Spearfishing in Southern N.S.W.* by Barry Andrewartha and Robin Montcalm; and *Australian Seashores* by Isobel Bennett.

Thanks to Kevin Pearson for his editorial assistance.

Contents

CABRAMATTA   3
CUDMIRRAH
  Size of the Tide   15
  Physalia   17
  Sand-skiing   18
  Rockpools Referred To and Illustrated   19
  Crustacea   21
  Cudmirrah   22
  Sea Cells   24
  Parrot Fish   25
  Bathymetric Chart   26
  Cunjevoi   27
  Sea Tulips   28
  The Swimmer   29
  Pieta   30
  Three Structures   31
  Trace Elements   33
  The Red Tide   35
  Ekman Spiral   36
  Amongst the most picturesque molluscs of our rocky ocean shores are the chitons   37
  A Question   38
  Estuary   39
  Wreck of the Walter Hood   41
  Headland   44
  Dunes   46
  Ballad of a Spearfisherman   47
  Thermocline   49
  Sponge   50

Sea Eagles	51
Stingray	52
The Green House	53
Dementia	54
Dictionary	56
The Drift	57
Lighthouse	58
Swan Lake	59
Electra	60
It's Late	62
Grasses Will Not Fly	64
I Am Most Happy	65
The Same Poem	66
Triton	67
A Photograph	68
False Limpets and Their Relatives	69

CABRAMATTA

CABRAMATTA

*

in myxomatotic crystal balls
farmers saw the flexing virus
of the universe exercise its fist
in a rabbit's eye gone white and blind

....beneath dusty gums, afternoons
on the porches, in the fields
of dumped rusty cars
culling dreams the dirt farmers dreamed

and where else could sydney go
but up through the beach-blue clouds
north to gosford, south to woollongong
or west across the rabbit lands?

*

travelling now for years
without arriving at the place you left
you can't arrive because it's gone
and possibly did not exist- and, so
adaptably, you take the new version
of the hume highway as it slices
towards cambelltown obliterating
the older road that twisted down
through the razorback hills
you drive away from a huge monocytic
sun setting somewhere behind you
but that's not what you see
you see the new-estates
young families have photocopied
from a jennings-billboard you see thickening inching brick

like a child seamlessly growing
like a child you notice has changed
only when you've been away

you notice how the suburbs have developed
breasts and muscles, pubic parks
a need to be themselves

bulldozers experiment upon the horizon
they have widened the road
to make it fast and safe but
from the cut hills a milky juice exudes
sugars, smoke, oil, caoutchouc
the bodily fluids of houses

part window, part tendon
automatic as the fairlane gears
life accelerates
you smell sydney
you smell it coming
its mirage oil swims on the tar

but this isn't how you remember it
now that the highway by-passes
everything that is ordinary
you see only the ordinary invisibility of speed
you are unsure which cows
are trees, which trees are people
the anabolic blur flattens the lot
until you are driving fast into your own history
and digging deep into the eye within
which is the only place you see it

*

somewhere out here, my grandfather's body
lies in the chaste dirt, beyond camden church
beyond hospital and mossy stone

shards of lorry-rubber litter the verge
and you're not sure whether that clump of gorse
which passed like a real thing was after all
the approximate place where your cousin's mazda

slipped like paper beneath a truck
the old adolescence was dangerous
but the new one stretches like laudanum smoothing
out the ruts and edges, taking from you what lies
buried in the hills - and how can a car resist
the road's scar, the dicotyledon, the system
of intercellular spaces opening to the atmosphere
committing the homology of bones and rabbits
to inconsequence - this road flattens
sterilises everything - an efficient
movement of cartilage, stretch of vocal cord
even the wind can't alter the pitch of its voice

*

I drive into liverpool past the pizza hut
that was my father's motor-bike shop
they say my mother rode side-car
and that I did, too, as a baby
born with scrambler mud in her blood
and a taste of leather in her bottle-milky mouth

*I'm tougher than you
you're just a puss from pymble
a kelp-head from palm beach*
it was that kind of racism followed
you along wakehurst parkway
mona vale rd to narrabeen surf club
where the rich boys used words like
*what's the matter with you, westie
you frigid?*

*

at bathurst races, side-car riders
screamed their shoulders across tar
their bodies sending up sparks

I saw a man decapitated by the guard-rail
and from the corner of my eye I watched

a bikie gang called the rats, each a silver-studded
dirty-jeaned, black-booted grizzly
gulping beer as they lounged over petrol tanks
like they were shiny young bulls

you had to be over fifty to belong to the rats
my father told me
it was about then he sold the shop
sick of bikers
who took out a norton
for a test run and never came back

in the photo: sandown, 1950
a young man's elemental mud
my father scrambling
in sepia style he lays the bike on its coccyx
it rears like a horse

    *

a fibro history of cabramattan colloquialisms:
she'll be right mate; tom flipperies scrawl
across a toilet block's scarlet cape of brick

my grandmother serves tea on a plastic cloth

cousins grizzle their fairlanes
towards homebush for an unlawful drag
... the midnight track at brickies

and I'm driving
through the outskirts of sydney
numb as the best boyfriends
I met on the cb radio: it's King John here
calling for a copy
you flick I'll switch
go down Brother Butch...

vowel-static, it's a voice
you speak when your car's a burrow
in here you breed
inflamed around the eyes
going with the green
stopping with the red

thonged-foot flat to the floor
you blast the orange

your furry dice swing

    *

like everything else, you
resemble bits of socialism
bits of like and as though you were down to earth
but mostly you made a meal of petrol
fumes multiplying
within the cul-de-sac
within the cul-de-sac

even though you've been to university
presently you'll sling a couple of girlfriends
across the front seat
attack the gears, the column shift
like a woman
you'll turn right or left
for the sake of the curb
follow your instinct, get lost
and argue with the navigator
who is also you - scrambler child
whose brave days are obsolete

    *

petrol rivers
fume towards parramatta
pleistocene chimneys
smoke the sky-line: missus p missus a missus rra…

the traffic jams
same old factory spit! same old jail!

it's 1968 - an easter parade -
perhaps it's christmas -
each cardboard castle on wheels
is a huge green grassy america

bagpipes puff their cheeks
and strut ahead of the rsl mermaid
who, swathed in a mesh-metal suit
made of cola ring-top pulls
floats on a papier-mâché sea

espaliered children cheer

in two-four time bikes and chicks
grumble down main street six apace

missus p missus a missus rra
same old factory spit, same old jail!

around the corner comes a woman
on the prow of a ship, around the corner
comes miss parramatta; from poland; from
croatia; vietnamese, blonde

and, behind, the marching girls
in perfect step
trample the streamers and shake a little stick

*

you have nothing to say
except you loved the granville boys, their breath
like diesels, their hands slicking starships out of smoke

missus p missus a missus rra
missus m missus a missus tta
they could mousse you on the dance-floor
their crotches pressed to yours
they could stroke your hair
and you'd be hanging off the exhaust
their eyes looking right through you
as though you were the exhaust

every where you went
their virulence followed you
like a thrilling disastrous dare

the men I love still have perfect voice
a carburetter, idling to be lit
flicking to a rev-head beat:
go down Brother Butch
go down Brother Butch
go sweet

*

so you've cut your hair thinking
no one will recognise you
but your hair's always been unsure of itself
perms rained through
with grandmothers, pick-up-sticks, foam rollers
coloured purple like cabramatta on a hazy day

ceramic ducks fly by trifecta on the wall
the plastic roses smell of tripe
cigarettes bitch the gossipy air

she married the strobe
he blew out the tyres of her eyes
next day she's back on the dance-floor
white teeth matching her underwear

white knickers through white jeans
I've always liked dancing in a circle
with my girlfriends
you might say it's as close as you ever get
to the jungle

*

behind the wheel
you know where you are going
you confabulate yourself
into the fast/slow flow
of the city's irritable blood

you give the finger
cut the map off at the corner

and remember your aunt
pouring her accident compensation money
coin by coin into the poker's till...
something in the rhythmical pull -
the old-fashioned lever, hard
as a crucifix in her hand -
the queen of diamonds
the jack of clubs, the four tropical fruits in a row -
just like that other church where the chasuble
changes colour with the seasons - her fingers
dripped their habit in a plate

*

at the family reunion in lidcombe park
all the girls wear big hair and name tags
because we've bred like razorback rabbits
just like grandma taught us

even if we were to blame
we'd have another spin on the pokies
a jackpot, like a funeral, is talked about for days

you stand around in the sun -
you say which one is this, god he's grown -

even though you've been away eleven years
you were christened yesterday

and absent, again, beneath shadowy trees
you understand the wish

the wish to touch the root
which is the tree. All lies begin
with identity, confusion, clarity.

  *

cars sit in the car-sale yards
along parra road like books
in a shiny store

and you know how the harbour
plumps up in the afternoons
touching the west with rabbits' breath

but, now, what of the future
and who do I love?

the minute I put a key
in the ignition
a word on a page
I feel the engine strip down...

remove the muffler
paint a sunset on the hood
switch on the radio

and the rhythm of your words
finds you pronouncing what you know:

it's King John here calling for a copy
you flick I'll switch
go down Brother Butch
go down Brother Butch
go sweet

CUDMIRRAH

Size of the Tide

Fevers confuse; lucidities break.
Cudmirrah plays hide and seek
with my mind. Now I remember
now I forget - this isn't a game
nor yet a death. Grandchildren
come out! Come out of the fire!
The plover is wintering here.
In the bays of my name, I
taste a river; slightly curved
at tip, I have borrowed a cliff.
I arrive September. Do you know
where I am? I am chasing
the flame which travels
the thought; I am chasing
the stone-coloured eggs of birth
through smaller, smaller sparks.
I can't speak of spheres, of worlds
I haven't seen, but I've seen the unseen
as it floods and spills
uncontained by the walls of sand
time has built around my tongue.
I've taught you to float.
I've taught you to fish from a wooden boat.
You've lassoed the air above my head
and cast your lines long -
but you can't make me wake
or make yourself known.
Memory
digs less for an accurate world
than for the fetch of the wave
and the tide which calls my name
most faintly inwards.

When your heels dig deep in the bed
I see molluscs, pipis, hives in the sand.
I see the neap tide's quarter-moon
diminished, dry-boned as chalk.

I see fresh bait in your mind each dawn.
I see nets and gutting and food.
I see the shape of shells, the surnames of jetties
and the habits of South Coast birds.

I see you swivelling the edge of Cudmirrah:
stars, delicate colonies, filling the darkness
where your heels have left a hole.
I see the full moon, red as cinnabar

rise over Berrara point and carve
the rollocks of a quiet boat with quiet light.
When your heels dig deep in the bed
I see that pain has infinite memory.

I see you unable to comb your hair
the mudflats matted, empty, anywhere.
Adrift, I see your fingers plucking
as though at flowers on your skin.

You won't find a vase to put love in.
Your riddles of salt can't choose
or change or decide my mind.
Don't tell me the world is content.

I'm sailing this dune through a dark-scarp
light, the only one of its kind.
Even now you can't see me
through the bars of this body, my shell.

It's careless how memory takes shape
falls apart - but see - the boats - coming
across the bar? Hurry. The men are coming home!
As if from war, not fishing.

Physalia

A northeaster has flown in
bringing hundreds of glistening sacs
Portugese men-o'-war
with threads of crotch-blue hair
camouflaged blue
against a grass-green sea.

This is the way we stepped
between stings
popping the bladders flat
with our sticks
a bright blue skin
teaching me the first remedy
of sand - quick! rub it in quick
don't cry.

All of yesterday was
a blue mood
and suddenly I think of cousins
their oblique, transparent voices
tangling with lines
Velella velella: "By the Wind Sailors"....

I dream of an island at night
a blue lady... eyes bright; listening
her tentacles...
shh *porpita porpita* - smaller than a daughter.
Such strings drawn out.
Offshore. Driven in.

Sand-skiing

In Sussex Inlet
above the blackfish shores
my grandparents loved
beyond El Alamein's thin beach
towards Cudmirrah point, steep cliffs
hang down from the military holiday camp
hidden high in the scrub.
Down these dunes
we skied on planks of packing wood
rubbed smooth with candle grease.
Down into ice-green water we flew.
Went under. Showered back.
And took the view, named
for a battle we knew nothing about
back up the slope we'd marked
with ti-tree branches, slalom crosses.
Opposite, mudflats steamed
their estuarine brew: silver gulls
cormorants; weedbanks, darkening
as the morning grew bright, lay
beneath the river's shuffled skin.
Don't think we were young;
we weren't anything at all.
We were - as the "hinge of fate"
happens to be - as the wind is -
rushing through the blur of rushing.
We were carving the line of our time
down a powdery face.
I'll race you. Be first. First bird
to rip still water apart.
From Miteiriya ridge
to Rahman (all do and all don't)
all day we climbed, died, climbed
until the tide lay like a wrung towel
against the cliff's yellow snow
and the sun, going down
showered back.

Rockpools Referred To and Illustrated

I lie in weedy cellos
strung along the shore's pocked fringe.
I lie in rockpools.
I lie in their soft cloth.

I lie between backshore
and foreshore (as though between
the pages of a scarcely remembered
oceanography book)

recalling the shells I found as a child
at Bherwherre. The jingle shells
were pious as eucharists
ruffled waifs they worked

the salty crevices
their pale Irish habit fouling
the keels of boats swaying at anchor.
And tapestry cockles

with vestments of Florence
oceanic scribbled faces
and waistcoats from Portugal
lips from a brothel, burrowed

through the sand's wash
into the skin beneath the shallows
.....and *Tellina roseola*
the pink butterfly shell

arrived intact once per childhood
its porcelain leaf-ear
pierced by a precise jeweller
the carnivorous sand-snail.

In the rockpool, a gestalt takes place.
People are passing from house
to house, from street to street.
Memory here casts a spell

and the rockpool is captured by it
- the swimmers, fish and crabs
the broken membranes
the tangled fibrils

are imperfections laid out
beneath the sky for touching.
I lie in rockpools. They fill and spill
and lose their separateness.

They are boring now. All the same.
No wing to match the first wing.
Skeletons, shells lie in hard cloth.
It depends what you see when you look.

Crustacea

Cudmirrah's night crabs
italicise the sand, busy
minute volcanoes, their infinites
of burrowing *must*
make a home just where I am
sideways in circles

not an army
but a tough, timid carapace
of nippered hands
individual plans

leave me alone
they might be saying
as they scatter across the tideline
like nimble ghosts
disturbed by the footsteps
of birds or children

the hermit crab
is too fragile to exist
without the loan of some other
animal's shell

slender hooks
hold on to an ideal self
but what do we know
of our own self's wealth?

we move forwards or sideways
around you grandmother
our bodies are
drab white; young, rusty brown

in our family
we don't often lament
we are usually busy
which is how we fear death

Cudmirrah

I

Cudmirrah's slow foam stretches towards
Red Head, Green Island and the mouth
of Lake Conjola to the south. Reefs thrust
from the sea-bed; kelp cliffs plummeting
temperately down to where the schoolfish
of summer- Tuna, Kingies and Salmon -
feed in the evenings. Across the beach
fishermen walk alone or in pairs; they carry
antennae, fibreglass rods, eyes which swing
from their hands. Strange woolly insects
leaving canvas testicles of bait clumped along
the shore, they wade thigh-deep through surf
as if through liquid grass. My grandmother walks
backwards shielding her face from the sand.
The lines, behind her, strain towards breaking.

II

Stars arrange familiar constellations
into that one inquisitive light
whose peculiar aura is said to beckon
the mind down its last nostalgic tunnel.
The sea here is narrow, so straight
you can see mile upon mile of shameless
wave-flowers criss-crossing the currents
which build only to build again what Babel
built on dreams. The beach, garnet-eyed
with driftwood fires, weeps between paws
of rock and the moon hangs in a wise corner.
Spray hisses and the landscape rises on
hind legs as though preparing to mate with
the wind's feral herds. The milky palate
shines, high-arched, over fountains.

III
My brother has buried me in a play coffin;
my head above the sand, my body below.
It wasn't me; it was a damsel let him do it
and now she calls from the tomb's parapet:
Come back St George! Come back! Chivalrous
as a man who has won he walks away and
leaves her swallowed, until more teasing than
cruel he digs her up with a plastic spade like a sand-eel.
The verisimilitudes of play and war, sea
and sand are siblings without an inch
of give between them. The younger loves the older
for his: let's do whatever we want
and the older loves the younger because
she loves him fully. Each will fight the nature
they have buried in the other.

IV
How do we choose the places we love?
First we love, then we choose. Or call it love
later, when memories assume
the cloudiness of the past. Recollected faces
wander landlessly, enviously
between past and present. Present faces are
overlooked until they threaten to become the past.
Or else all places and people in them
are soliloquil aspects of an enormous silence.
Fisherman fish for the night that swims
for the cold-blooded hunger. Already I confuse
what I am looking for among the dissipating
forms of the waves. Lorca said
" the loved one sleeps on the poet's breast."
I plant my feet like native trees and whisper Cudmirrah.

Sea Cells

Water parts, folds
and folds again: embroideries
Nereids, spray.

Deeper than Jacques Cousteau's
subliminal seapods
deeper than Precontinent III
built upon the self-contained lung
of aqua worlds untouched by surface misery
cells, marionettes
enact their "luck of the sea"
their special script
a set-piece, tableau of jetties
DNA: nothing flat, or altered.

Hazily, she turns to drift
this grip of suck
and scale

but lazily she drifts, this fish:
Pacific, plasmic, mild.

Parrot Fish

Light temperature salinity -
careful words of pitch and tone

grandmother, there is something
to remember before you go

viscosity
resistance, flow

turbulence, capacity
the easy words are factory words

parrot fish are chewing up the coral
turtles have left the bay

but - light temperature salinity -
our bonds are not those of ice

we can rotate with little
or no restriction

we change course
about once per second.

Bathymetric Chart

A pulse transmitted
by a transducer on the hull of a ship
reflects the ocean floor.

By taking half the time elapsed
between pulse and echo

multiplying that
by the speed of sound
and recording the profile
of the so sounded shadow

the depth of a life is calculated.
In which chart are your schemas?
Your soundings are dipping
for earlier, earlier memories
- you are a sales girl now
at Angie H. Halls general store
in Macksville 1927.
Phone number: 3.
Box number: 4.
Merchant for drapery, mercery, boots & shoes
grocery, ironmongery, crockery, furniture
and produce.
I know you're there
because you whisper to no one
Halls for All...Halls for All...

You are, this moment, praised
for the excellent knowledge you have of the business.

Cunjevoi

I want less frailty
Nature knows what I mean

like people, the creatures of the sea
have proper names and nicknames:

ascidians, sea-squirts, chordates
cunjevoi

the backboneless primitives
cluster along Cudmirrah's shoulders

each has a rudimentary brain
an eye-spot, a mouth and an anus

each can breathe and feel
the foot which presses the sea from their bellies

their generic name, Tunicata, recalls
the shapeless garment Aristotle described

they are tough, these porridges
they survive the battering of time

they have filtered centuries of sediment
through orifices of abbe-like calm

attached as adults to rocks
(as children, for a few hours free)

they drink the sea through a thousand gill-slits
and wash up after storms as tulips.

Sea Tulips

Sea tulips actually look like potatoes
small unpeeled earthy potatoes
at the end of a stalk
under the wharf
or clumped along the rocks
at low-tide.

Hermit crabs are not lonely
nor fiddler crabs musical.

The snapping prawn
won't hurt a fly
and the elephant-snail is tiny.

Alzheimer's disease
does not correctly name
estuaries
torn from visceral moss.

We place so much
in the hands of strangers
so as not to be confused with razor shells
or sentiments.

The Swimmer

Swimming through words
with no fixed point
one with the elements, unclear

head down, breathing side to side
I enter the fishbowl's mind.
Aquarium - private fragmentary world.
Shapes and colours speak
of references that drift and sting and glide.
My ears are filled with water's
soundless thinking.
My mouth
now, a place for breathing.

If I picture absence
the beach off season
I am alone: this is mine
this ocean all around a continent
the pleasure of waves like mullet.

I swim away from scenes
remembered as salt across windows
clouds massed in the sky
the possibilities of spray.

Nobody for miles. I feel fine.

I am cutting, free-style,
across a dream.
Naive indulgent lady
no do not touch me sea!
I flex my fins as muscles
and the cradle of being
is as quiet as a skull.

Pieta

Your hair so soft - from it
I wash the day's salt
with a bowl of tankwater.
Now you wash mine
and we drink from the spigot
tasting the clean rain
you ration out in cups and pots.
Softly, too, fire burns in the sun
and the air speaks
through the wings of diving birds.

Three knowledges are these:
water fire air
but now, years later,
of these elements perhaps
you value only air
as softly conscious
you curl your body
around an ear of earth
and cradled by the Infant death
ask: will I / won't I
leave?

Three Structures

Formlessness I will divide.
From decay will be growth.

Climate will fit the design.
You will not fall between the boats.

Here is the text
the oceanographer's map:

behind are the mind's
suspicious zones

ahead lies the ocean's
three-layered structure

each a different colour
each a careful graph:

1. the surface 2. the pycnocline
and 3. the dark isolate mass

below each poem
where sun cannot scatter its spectrums

and the Great White, austere as a ghost
slips across a shadowless floor.

The surface reflects
an idea, a ceiling

made of words and names
and tidal countenances;

the pycnocline is a doublefold
of toughened skin

which feels and repels sadness;
and the deep ocean, scarcely moving

is a tail which keeps its balance
by all that is balanced upon it.

Trace Elements

Six elements comprise more than 99%
of sea-salts: chlorine; sodium;
magnesium; calcium; potassium; sulphur.
Ocean waters are well-mixed.

The surface is blue, shallow or grey
but the deepest blues
mark those regions devoid of plankton
which are dense, without life.

The deepest blues are the deserts
the calcareous Saharas
where ships and terrified bronzes
twist like windmills
as they sink with open-eyes

and even as they sink
rise alive from fables.

I'm a woman of layers
sand and rewritings.
Cycled by currents
illogical breezes

from the daily heating and cooling
of love
(elements of love: past place;
passed present;
passing now as it passes
now present)

the net gain is love
its abundance: the red tide

near the coasts of my heart.
But what has happened?
Was something taken?
By whom?
And what did I say?

The Red Tide

These worms swim beautifully
undulating the sides of their body's
kimono - jet black, white, pink
and orange they prey on the ocean's
almost dead, making slime
as they wrap themselves around their prey

they are the spiders of the sea

living beneath stones

their feathered plumes
penetrating the blood vessels
of gulls ducks and pelicans

holding fast to seaweeds
burrowing into the sleek mud of estuaries
secreting their homes behind them

flat leaf-like transparent beings

once grasped, we
discretely fear our natures

we lift the weed and skim the stones
and circle back
the way we've come.

Ekman Spiral

Spirals of energy
extend a hundred meters downwards
a kind of laminar flow of pages
sliding across each other

long days
spent browsing the minute bookstores
of rocky shores...

half nylon
worlds glinting, cilial tangles...

lineal, arrowed, inept
energy flows
and the gyre folds back
upon the past of its trace
creating the flowchart
of a permanent self
undeflected by continents

eavesdropping salt
I pour the sea from cup to cup
so that we
might exist there, briefly, in the pouring

a vast furrowed tongue
licks the break wall

the fact is you forget me
layer by layer
going down stairs
in the awful dark.

Amongst the most picturesque molluscs of our rocky ocean shores are the chitons

Facts seek to be more than handsome
than uncertain words
but fictions, contradictions
supersede and erode their stature.

Chitons are subdued
by a broad leathery armour.

Like facts, they are symmetrical creatures
crawling slowly by means of a muscular
elongating foot

and when blazed by lowtide sun
they drop off towards the shady side of knowledge
with the gliding movement of a snake.

A Question

What is satisfaction?
If a woman about to love
thinks of elsewhere islands
she is foolish.
To remain alive, anticipatory
unafraid of auguries
she must bathe in deep waters.
She must be thrown from the jetty
and feel the cobwebbed weeds
reach for her ankles. She must
swim with thrashing strokes to shore
where her mother waits with young eyes.
She must watch the heart urchin's
desert tracks in the sand
and be as alive at night as she is when desired.
She must be embedded in
or partly covered by sand
so that when she opens sublittoral doors
she receives the sea that is due.

Estuary

I

Across the estuary
our aluminium Topper
trails a burly of birds.

Sit down or you'll capsize the boat.
Sit down. Or we'll throw you over.
There's sharks in here. They'll get you.

Pass me the mullet and the knife and bread.
Give me the poddy trap.
Sit down Paul.
Don't touch the toad fish.
Its spikes are poisonous.

Pull up anchor.
The fish aren't biting here.
Let's go to the mangroves.

II

He's capsized the boat!
The motor's sunk like a penny in a well.
My jeans are heavy as metal.
I'm almost walking through water to shore
dragging the boat by its tow rope.

As Steve dives for the motor
we sit on the edge of the mudflat
watching a man
pump yabbies from their holes.

Soon my grandmother is clapping her hands
on the other side of the river.
She's been watching us through the window
with binoculars
and carries an armful of dry clothes.

III

At the end of the jetty
I see weeds shivering
beaks of silver-finned bream.

Oysters, bronze anklets
wind their slow succulent chains
up the pylons.

Some shells are white
as winter moons, easy
fruit plucked by gutting knives.

Others are black as the oyster-catcher
wading with the other wading birds
in the sleeves of the sun.

And this voice mirrah mirrah
bone wind
which blows around the estuary's headlands
older than anchors tugging
the ocean's floor

this mirrah
is the arcane sound
around which
my waves fold their forms.

I climb the path
within my grandmother's forehead

from which cliff
the view has moved
a short distance

from which view
the rips extend two or three kilometres
and then, as though bored
or relieved, end.

Wreck of the Walter Hood

Cut from highland trees I was built in Aberdeen
and made into a clipper queen.
Singing shreds of Nordic wrecks
from that laced bodice of Dartmouth port
through storms unseen and breaking still, I sailed
full swing past Gabo's lights and headed north
towards Jarvis Bay in New South Wales
where devil's spit kicks out upon the reef Berrara.

I race before a southerly storm, thick black
fog obscuring any signs of shore.
Ulladulla has blown away; by my calculation
we lose our way each time we plunge
the waterfalls of April. Upside down, sea-moan
screaming higher, Dear Latto steer me well,
deceive me with your confidence, in northern lands
Poseidon reigns - here, Pleiades, the Milky Way
climbs the sinews of Gidja moon.
No spirit I know, no *god save me* can pierce
the fire that snakes upon the reef Berrara.

So drum the wind, kilt the clouds!
Fly my thousand tons of dowl!
Dear Latto run the last of ninety sailing days
towards the harbour Sydney. The rain falls hard
across these decks and I must empty them
be quick! This shallow sea begins to smother me.
It hunts for pretty prey- and the wind unchecked does
surly pound my breast upon the reef Berrara!

My cabin-boy has snapped in two!
The wave dogs snarl a butchering blue!
I spill as though I'm birthing blood, bagpipe hull
now rip-and-splinter. Wine, beer, pickled pork
are bobbing from my belly. Sharks
with mossy fins of white and bronze

circle the men who try to swim for shore.
Dear Latto, where are you, my captain?
Have you, too, abandoned me upon the reef Berrara?

For three days, swollen, in delerium, I have chafed
upon a jagged tooth. Most of the crew are still aboard
clinging to my forehead. By the forlorn flame
of three wild moons they eat the coxswain's dog
and rawly shake with fever. Unkind providence!
On April 26th, that you begin a fresh unholy storm
and bring no hope to Englishmen upon the reef Berrara.

The wind has carved a path through clouds
where skims the Morning Star but *listen now, let go*
a spirit walks from mast to mast
and enters dreaming sand. A settler named
George Robinson has dreamed a nightmare
of my plight and roused Ulladulla town to find me.
Big Donelly swims the naked surf
and rescues nine more men through sharks and thrash
and frenzy. Donelly's arm is slashed but Latto
has washed up dead and still more timid men
will not leave my slender threads upon the reef Berrara.

Looters arrive with carts and hessian bags.
They cut off Latto's finger for his onyx ring.
(That stone is worn by one who'll die alone, unloved)
 - but cursed or not, fish ungutted, work undone
for seven days the coast is drunk
until, summoned by telegraph, the freighter Illawong
plucks the last half-starved from sore misbeating heart
as pyred by the embers of a calm dawn
I roll on rattled side and sink upon the reef Berrara.

Of my thirty five, fifteen died and were buried in
the sassafras - perhaps, perhaps not, with human
grace and naming prayer.
The wind next year uncovers their graves

bird bones, hand-wings, grit to grit - happy history!
They name this shore the Coast of Tragedy
but wrecked in mind alone, I head for home.
No lesson learned, the narrative has run aground.
No pity, please - dear Latto hear me well-
I linger whole in coral fish, in ballad ghost
my silent spine with weed entwined,
with Robinson and Donelly, upon the reef Berrara.

Headland

Locations change
as the sea rises and falls
but the headland remains
a stable form, a cleft tree
slowly felled
by an axe of water.

Each pebble falls
upon the rock-platform below
a field pitted with littorina
perriwinkles, Chinese hats.

The bombora cuts a white line
for three quarters of a mile offshore.
This may not be the place where the Hood went down

but the sun drowns
through clouds doused in shark's blood
and kerosene flame

and when the first star arrives
before the sun has gone and fishes of light
begin feeding from the moon's basket
it is the same sea beckons
the same salt bats from Karangamite caves.

And the wind which burns through me
as though my clothes are riggings
scutters my pores until I feel a salt
eat down to the bone to the spine

to the fishes they multiply
sting my eyes
sandy thorns.

There is a moon here
for every mood
a moth's white sail
a sky's purple moss.

Castaway, albino dragons
the waves have eyes
of mineral power

long stroking claws
stained with spices
blue and black theft.

A bird urge
wings outstretched....

almost a lover
the precipice sings
of blindfold, step and flight.

Dunes

Dunes reach inwards
into powder rooms
where voices muffled and trapped
slowly seduce the earth.

Dunes, pearl-pipes
sound out the voices of men and women
separated, their steps obliterated
by drifts of longing.

For faces unchanged beneath graves
the wind digs.
For faces reflected
the moon polishes the dune's silver.

Across the slipping face, rain weeps
sinks, but is not lost.
In the dune's dryness there is
a nomadic snow.

In the dune's shape
a dusty child settles
to sleep, dreaming
of breasts weaning the sea.

Ballad of a Spearfisherman

I'll tell you the story of an underneath day
the spear in my hand like a Kilibob man
flippered and quick
I've finned through the gardens of Babylon
the snake of my breath, pure rubber.

I'll tell you the story of an underneath day
diving with Gazza and Shane for Snapper
deep Sweep and metal-blue Crays
off Redhead, where the reef tumbles down
through sponges aflame, and forests unnamed
are lazy as pines, and Dories called John
press biblical skin to the barb of my thumb.

I'll tell you the story of an underneath day
where night once dawned in the shape of a fish-
shiver-deep as a breeze, the Whaler slipped in-
and circled my long-line limbs.
His corner-sly eyes were scarcely awake
but aggressive, sleek as a submarine
he flashed his chest: the scars of Dugong wars...

I'll tell you the story of an underneath day
bloody Gazza and Shane no where to be seen
I'm fetching my kill - this Groper is mine -
I 'm dragging the Groper out by the gills
when svelte as silk the Whaler flies in, grabs the dish
from my fist and swallows it sideways.

I'll tell you the story of an underneath day
where fins like falcons cruise in the gutters.
I've swum through the gardens of Babylon.
I've drunk the black ink of angry Squid

but, hey, if tomorrow is fine, I'll leave spear and
smokey behind - and follow that Whaler who took
my Groper down to his Bendalong maze.
Through marble-white boulders
I'll dive, killing nothing but a long bronze time.

Thermocline

There is this:
the ocean's thermocline
a fan of great stability
which holds to form the valleys
between waves, the waiting plains.

The mathematics, vectors of feeling
and weed equilibriate
where water becomes tense with depth.

Lying between the eye's horizon
and the eye's blindness
the thermocline hoards memories that do not fade

for without light, without heat
the sea would be an infinite homogenous
forgetting.

Cudmirrah Shoalhaven Swan Lake Ulladulla.

Waves are never one colour -
they inhabit space, not place -
they're in the sea's lung
then they're out in the open
mouthing the smoke of Bherwherre -

then they curve to the shore
taking the ship's dog with them.

Girls lie nearby
rubbing hot-noonday suns
into their skin's cool echo.
I must think of the wave as a diary.
Scarcely daring to read
what I have written the day before
in case I edit what I mean.

Sponge.

The bulk of a sponge is space
and sponge specialists are few.
Each sponge has a colony of cells
containing minute spicules of lime and silica
a system of canals and chambers
 so it is through a great palace
that water enters, circulates, passes
holds hands with delicate flagellae
for a moment opening eye-pores
to talk of small matters.
A piece of sponge, broken off
will grow into a sponge
or a bud will form
and brush the face quickly.
Forget those drab specimens
bottled in brine!
The live sponge is not easily
compressible.
I hear footsteps
upon 500 million year old cushions
of unconsciousness - half plant
half heliotrope - flower in me!
Soak me with pageants, life.

Sea Eagles

White breasted sea-eagles
circle the Hood
like huge butterflies.

Feeding on beach-washed eels and mullet
soaring in the pairs
of co-operative hunting

they enter the dreams of Robinson
and lead him skywards
to their nests of air.

See grandmother - we
are recording the swimmer
the cry, the unexplored X, coloured red

meaning this is where
we will go without finding
the village of strange implements and boasts.

There is a way of touching the dreams of another
of calling when you have no voice.
We make a tower from sticks
and hang it with feathers, funeral stones
rubber thongs, whelks, a wind-chime.

Stingray

Nothing is in its place. I alligator roll
through the dumper, come up
with sand in my mouth
the clean grit of summer.
These grains, sharp crystals
irritate the skin
until everything fluid
grinds in the groyne of my mind
a pocket, now a fracture
swept apart by imagery.

Black Drummer. Black Cod. San Souci Dolphin.
On a good day, Mnemosyne sees
clear to the trilobites ten fathoms down.
Nights are for busters, the bruising of rain.
How easily Stingrays camouflage
themselves in the sand, she said later
striking out for the channel, forgetting her name.

The Green House

Rain slicks the highway
between Sydney and Sussex Inlet.
At Kiama the blowhole
boils like an old woman's kettle.
Everything seems to be in its place
even my father pointing to the totem pole
of available motels as we turn from the highway.
We stir in the back of the car and stretch our legs.
At midnight the town sleeps.
A kangaroo's carcass peers into headlights.
The silver boat-shed is in its place.
The camping ground is in its place.
Stretched beside a mile of dark river
dead caravans pass by - until
turning the corner of Mrs Phillip's mansion
I come to the green house (screen memory, etcetera).
Missing pieces of scrabble.
Napthalene, musk, apple-spice.
Folded sails, stale bait, lobster pots.
We arrive to do. Relax by doing.
Outside in the garden, two
tanks brim with rain
water still drumming
but gently now on iron roof and door.

Dementia

I

The child arrived yesterday from a city's black liver.
The whole house is open, direction
a shovelled castle, limp as kelp on the beach.
I bend at rock-pools
in rhythm with my grandmother
who wears a yellow hat
who stands now with hands behind her back
watching the morning disappear
the eyebrows of clouds
lifting over the sun's monacle.

II

Banded sand shell
Bankivia fasciata
thousands of sand dwellers
with delicate bands of
white, pink and brown

too many to count or hold
refugees, they wander
through the wash's lost strength
and nurse like cocoons
at the air.

III

How the triolet ends I can't tell
Alice Bentley, Alice Ware.
Repetitions weave a fixing spell.
How the triolet ends I can't tell.
Alice Bentley, Alice Ware.
In pairs, flocks of mal de mer...
How the triolet ends I can't tell.
Alice Bentley, Alice Ware.

IV
It is a brief poem of sparse rhyme.
The boundaries are defiant
only in me.

Your body has outgrown
three languages: terza rima, science,
memory; let's move to another town.

Dictionary

Giant waves are generated by sudden
slumping of the ocean floor.
Called tsunamis, sometimes
tidal waves
they are unrelated to tides.

Wind waves are the ripples
the nipples capillaried and tense
which blow across still mirrors.

Progressive waves are the trains
across which passenger corks
travel forwards with the crest
backwards with the trough.

The stationary wave
or weedy seich slops side to side
across St George's basin.

Tides are the very long waves
stretched between vowels.

Five miles out, what can I see?
I see an eclipse, an eerie shroud.
I fill it with all I nothingly know.

The Drift

Jelly fish head for the bottom
when a cold change comes

they drift more silently
than combs through hair.

A mudworm festers
the oyster and spoils the harvest;

we built a cannery at Narooma
even though the Wagonga salmon

no longer enter that river.
We drift in circles.

In 1827 Thomas Florence
named St George's basin

and discarded the native name
Bherwherree: to hurry.

We drift in the margins
of brother, sister, mother, father.

The drift has no purpose that I can see
but I name the waves

and sort their forms and measure
their distances, their curves and sines.

No sign of a pepsi-drinking moon
but straw-holes pierce our atmosphere.

Satellites drift above, more loudly
than combs through hair.

Lighthouse

At Perpendicular Point, the lighthouse
shuts, opens upon ebb and flow -
the same damned if I will, damned if I won't
be consistent in love or self.
A stubborn molecule, a rudderless thing
steers process from here to there
to here where I pivot through words like a doll
on a stick or a pencil. I'm sifting through
debris the way the Illawarra Steam Company
sifted skeletons from Moruya bar:
Monaro, Kameruka, Benandra, SS Trident.
How exactly does a storm grind a wreck into its blood?
It breaks the back sagging the belly.
It breaks again forward of the bridge
spreading flotsam from Durras to Bateman's Bay
while at Perpendicular Point, the kerosene dragon blinks
not hearing anything but the fog on its eyelid.

Swan Lake

Swan Lake ablaze with prawning lanterns.
My father drags the longest
and strongest until his net is full.
Women in their place on the bank
with the filleting knifes and the baskets
kids somewhere in the shallows
caught between androgeny and driftwood.
The wind rises. Peter is bitten by a fortesque.
The sandflies are silent.
My father drags again through the weeds.
I will be manly, waiting for him
until everyone's gone with their buckets.
I'll carry the other side of his net
through the middened darkness.
Help me sprinkle the catch with salt
he'll say - but I won't look
at prawns blushing, hissing in a pot.
I'll never eat prawns again
their shells like empty cupboards
stink of dead cats.

But as he eats the sweet meat
of the sea with lemon
I watch my father's arms rest on the table
then sleep in stringless nets
which haul and fish and let me go.

Electra

I walk the dirt roads with my cousin.
Boys whistle only at her
but she wants me to walk with her all the time.
She won't go alone to the beach or the shop.

Along Cudmirrah's paths and to the movies
we walk arm in arm
counting the whistles on all her fingers.
I'd prefer to be talking with Moss

in his rattle-trap caravan
about the ships big as black meadows
which, all along the reef, tilt into silt.
I tell Moss that a dog dreams

flat on his back
flat, docile, but sharp in his bones.
Sometimes I sleep like a drowned river,
I say, and sometimes on a precipice

a falling into or away from.
Sometimes I sleep like a one-eyed gull
swooping from a clifftop down
to submarine canyons of fish.

(I can't imagine how bored he was)
but sometimes, I say, I dream
flat on my back, as an animal does, and
hundreds of kingfish swim in fertile pairs

gliding over wrecks where gold coins
dance in the fists of statues
and anchors rust in anonymous caverns.
These are the ballrooms where no rules dance

Moss says, and he calls me Electra.
I tag alongside my cousin
watching the Pointers, the surfing boys circle
her urn-bright nipples, and dream of being older.

It's Late

It's late and I've come to the beach
to walk beneath the moon's rag.

A fisherman is walking home.
His rod dips and nods as though divining
treasure in the kelp-soured air.

Too old for games
he lands each step in another's
as though it is his mother's footprints

he follows, and by changing the shape of her trace
leaves his own life-line
scrawled across the sand's palm.

Now, the fisherman walks quickly
and then too slowly, as though unsure
of his destination, or of the silence
he lingeringly leaves.

Moss Wickum said
that every fisherman is unhappy with his catch
and most happy when he has caught nothing.

I have remembered this or else
I've constructed its truth
from nothing, myself.

Once I watched a diver bring abalone
to the surface
and cut them open until ten violet shells
reflected the sky -
then the fisherman (was it my brother?)
left the beach
the way a child leaves his mother or father

looking ahead
as ruined shells envelop the sea
and the light begins to dry over
all that will be abandoned differently.

Grasses Will Not Fly

Trousers billowing.
Wigs of tussock fly from their perches.
The sea floor spreads
leaving the footprints of continents behind.
Black basalt footprints
fractional, pre-school size.

In shallow places
foraminifers
the one-celled parasites
sheathe and eat the ocean's junk-
not a weapon to be found
here, among the hours.

When the fisherman left the beach
he left pig flower, ti tree, stunted wattle.
He left the slit mullet curing in the sun.
He tracked across the dune I could not see -
Cudmirrah which has nothing to do with place
nor with people. Cudmirrah of closed eyes
and totems, Cudmirrah concerned
with the body's territory of revisions
copper transcriptions, with chance
and the dream-dragons which rise
through ribs of devouring mutant matter
to the cliff where I am lately
with my salt palaces and vespers.
My grasses will not fly under their own impetus.

I Am Most Happy

I am most happy watching the shape of the land.
The past begins at random, not planned.
I open my eyes. I'm stung with sand.
Love transcends our ability to understand.

The past begins at random, not planned.
I feel what is held grow smaller here.
Love transcends our ability to understand.
You are faceless my beach, disappear.

I feel what is held grow smaller - here
I reach for shadows, for fragments. Again
You are faceless my beach, disappear.
Shells have dreams, the familiar no name.

I reach for shadows, for fragments again.
We become whole when reflected upon and held.
Shells have dreams, the familiar no name.
This is the world. This is the world.

We become whole when reflected upon and held.
In the dark, I obey no command.
This is the world. This is the world.
I am most happy watching the shape of the land.

The Same Poem

I see the same poem in rivers and pores
in things shaped by glass and bowls.
I see the same poem in fact, folk-lore

in footnotes, religion, metaphor.
Stars sparkle on a blue lapel, cold
as that brooch, the moon, and that tooth, the shore.

Gilding can't last can't touch the roar
of the sea's violent soul.
I see the same poem fold back on itself, but more

than this, I see disease-cure-cure. Children call
from the water: Come, mend the bodily earth. Whole
and in parts, we are surface, deep swell - all

we touch exists in the mind, outside the mind's law.
Poems can be done better but the sea consoles
what I break. I see the same poem in rivers
and pores. In things shaped by glass and bowls.

Triton

She holds the conch to my ear
and I hear its spiralling music
hack back to the pulse.
Lure of the tongue, the ear
another's calves tangled with mine....
the scale of love hacks back to the limit.
The female limit.
The perpetually pausing antique moment
which is a heart no bigger than the ruby
in a fish, in the roe, in the egg.
Knock-kneed, damaged heart, the whole
fire in the glass. I give the heart
a nipple stiff as a starfish.
I give the friable fist in the chest a lovely beat
and take you shining, dark, carved triton
back up the hill
where the view reflects back
easily like stormwater.

A Photograph

Cyanin, zaffre, purple. Sea-grape. Green.
It's a mistake to split the breast open -
to take a handful of gut, the backbone
the severed head, the eyes
which stare sideways from the nose.
It's a mistake to put your hands in the gills
and pose for a photo.
How dark the air is
and flimsy, the flimsy lights.

The garnet eye of a fibro house
beckons the best helpless ship to shore.
The one dissolving child
heads home through bracken and fences
finding everything she thought was there
a kind of faith, completely whole
plucked from sharp-mouthed foam
thrown back as greenshank song
mollymawk. Silver gull.

False Limpets and Their Relatives

Sea-ear, abalone, ear-shell
paua, mantle, foot, pounded food
sea-opal, green-white, nacreous pearl -
cells dismember particularly
counting, shrieking as they go -
mutton-fish, ruber, visceral curl
rainbow-fissure, smooth girl -
cultivate this which cultivated me -
swimmer, caress
sea-ear, ear-shell, elegy.